Dedicated to all those who love our country

Land Rights

Samantha Wortelhock, *oil on canvas, brush and syringe. Artist's collection*

*Against the backdrop of the 'many heads' of Kata Tjuta, a kangaroo
boxes with a cow to reclaim his sacred land.*

THE SPIRIT OF MY COUNTRY

Paintings by
Samantha Wortelhock & Damien Naughton

Calligraphy by
Dave Wood

'My Country' by
Dorothea Mackellar

High on Eucalyptus

Damien Naughton, *oil on canvas, brush and syringe. Private collection USA*

The first koala Samantha encountered in the wild lived near her home in Byron Bay. She was touched by the way the intrepid creature had braved the dense rainforest in search of a gum tree. Damien dedicated this work to the koala. He hopes that it will encourage fellow koala lovers to plant the scribbly gum trees needed to keep these creatures alive.

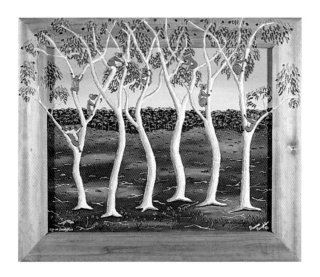

First in the series Australia–from the Heart
Produced exclusively for Australia Post

Other titles in the series:
The Bush, My Lover
Song of the Dreamtime

First published in Australia in 1994 by Fidado Pty Ltd ©
Poem copyright © The Estate of Dorothea Mackellar
Paintings copyright © Heaven & Earth Pty Ltd, 1994

National Library of Australia Cataloguing-in-Publication data:

Mackellar, Dorothea, 1885 - 1968.
The spirit of my country.
ISBN 1 875634 04 5
I. Wortelhock, Samantha. II. Naughton, Damien. III. Title.
(Series : Australia - from the heart; 1)
A821.2

Created and produced by Bruce Perry and Cecille Weldon
Editorial assistance: Linsay Knight, Leonie Draper
Design: Stan Lamond, Lamond Art and Design

Printed and bound in Australia by Griffin Press
Separations by Litho Platemakers

PREFACE

DOROTHEA MACKELLAR began writing 'My Country' as an impressionable 19-year-old far away from home. While visiting England with her parents, she felt overwhelmed by the need to express her deep love of Australia. Writing this poem was her way of doing this and it took her many years as she searched for images which would convey the essence of her country. During this time, Dorothea often found her opinions at odds with those of others around her.

> 'You are so lucky to be going home,' some told her.
>
> 'I'm not going home, I'm leaving home,' said Dorothea .....
>
> 'Oh, Dorothea,' said some who had travelled, 'don't you feel, when you come back, that the Heads are closing behind you like prison gates?'
>
> This attitude annoyed Dorothea.
>
> 'The Heads are the gates of my home,' she insisted, 'and I return through them with joy.'

Ironically, the poem was first published in a London magazine, *The Spectator*, in 1908 and only later reprinted in Australia in *The Call*. Its publication coincided with a growing sense of national pride, with Dorothea providing the words and images needed for others to express that pride.

In *Spirit of My Country*, first in the series Australia—from the Heart, Dorothea's poem is enhanced by the naive art of Samantha Wortelhock and Damien Naughton and the calligraphy of Dave Wood. Rather than reproducing a literal pictorial translation of the words, the paintings represent the contemporary nationalistic sentiments held dear by the artists, with images reflecting a concern for our unique natural environment.

Free Spirits

Samantha Wortelhock, *oil on canvas, brush and syringe. Sydney gallery*

This painting records Samantha's own experiences when, unable to take a holiday, she travelled to Lord Howe Island in a dream. It was so vivid that when she awoke she felt as if she really had been on holiday.

THE LOVE of FIELD AND COPPICE,
of GREEN AND SHADED LANES,
of ORDERED WOODS AND GARDENS
IS RUNNING IN YOUR VEINS,
STRONG LOVE of GREY-BLUE DISTANCE,
BROWN STREAMS AND SOFT, DIM SKIES
I KNOW, BUT CANNOT SHARE IT,
MY LOVE IS OTHERWISE.

Breakaway

Samantha Wortelhock, *oil on linen, brush and syringe. Sydney gallery*

The artist believes that humour is the most effective means of communication.
We take a whimsical break, away from reality, as seagulls trade places with
humans in this, the artist's most popular painting.

I LOVE A SUNBURNT COUNTRY, A LAND OF SWEEPING PLAINS

A Point of View

Samantha Wortelhock, *oil on canvas, brush and syringe. Private collection USA*

A dream inspired this vision of an untouched world where birds are the dominant species. The black cockatoo oversees its vast country from the ocean to the red centre. Gulls bake on the beach while their young nest in the treetops. Down below, black swans swim in the creek and emus strut amongst the desert spinifex. A wedge-tailed eagle clutches a little rabbit in its claws. Samantha believes that we could all benefit from seeing our world from such an objective viewpoint.

OF RAGGED
MOUNTAIN RANGES,
OF DROUGHTS
AND FLOODING RAINS.

Rest Assured

Damien Naughton, *oil on canvas, brush. Sydney gallery*

*Among the Sturt desert peas, saltbush and paper daisies, the great grey
kangaroo rests easily. With her highly unusual reproductive ability, she is able
to store a fertilised egg for future development while, at the same time,
nurturing both a newly born joey in her pouch and a young kangaroo at her
feet. This unique creature is certainly well equipped to survive in such a
harsh natural environment.*

I LOVE FAR HORIZONS,

Cod Almighty

Samantha Wortelhock, *oil on canvas, brush and syringe. Sydney gallery*

Despite their ominous appearance, the giant potato cod of the Great Barrier Reef are gentle creatures. With mouths gaping, they stare inquisitively at the human visitors to their tranquil world.

Playing with Time

Samantha Wortelhock, oil on canvas, brush and syringe. Sydney gallery

The artist was stimulated to paint this work after hearing that the rangers at Uluru had found eighty feral cats living in one tree. These feline killers destroy thousands of native marsupials each year. The cat holds a bilby between its jaws, playing with literally thousands of years of evolution.

AND HER BEAUTY
AND HER TERROR
THE WIDE
BROWNLAND
FOR ME

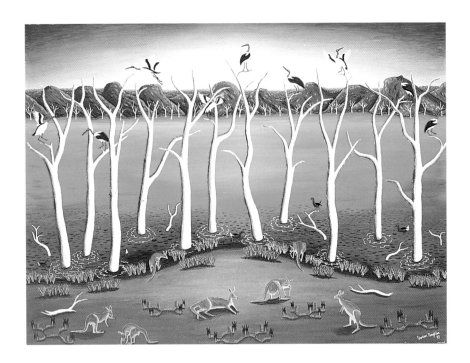

The Mighty Murray

Damien Naughton, *oil on canvas, brush and syringe. Sydney gallery*

*For hundreds of millions of years the fragile, tranquil beauty and perfect
rhythms of the "Mighty Murray" remained undisturbed. In just over one hundred
and fifty years, ignorance, arrogance and procrastination have all but killed
Australia's largest river. Such rivers are the vital arteries, the lifeblood, of our
planet. The artist finds it astonishing that we think we can change the course of
our rivers, misuse and abuse them, yet still expect them to
remain pure and untainted.*

THE STARK WHITE
RING-BARKED
FORESTS,
ALL TRAGIC TO
THE MOON,

My Dreaming Self

Samantha Wortelhock, *oil on canvas, brush and syringe. Private collection*

Inspired by a poem by Jane Roberts, this painting explores the possibility of being in two places at the same time — our dreaming self can travel while our physical body remains asleep in bed. Samantha believes that life has more dimensions than we can ever imagine.

My dreaming self lay on the bed
I stood aside in awe
'Why, Both of us are one'
I said, he said
'I thought you knew.'[2]

THE SAPPHIRE-MISTED MOUNTAINS, THE HOT GOLD HUSH OF NOON,

Fantassie

Samantha Wortelhock, *oil on canvas, brush and syringe.*

An artist has the ability to travel back into the past and show what might have been. In this painting, Tasmanian tigers abound on the earth. The work serves to remind us that it is too late to begin appreciating things once they have gone. This is particularly topical when we consider the current plight of the native bilby.

GREENTANGLE OF THE BRUSHES WHERE LITHE LIANAS COIL

Yin and Yang

Damien Naughton, *oil on canvas, brush and syringe. Sydney gallery*

*This work takes its name from the elemental principles of Chinese philosophy,
Yin and Yang. The artist shows the two principles side-by-side in nature,
represented by the assertive magpie (Yang) and the passive wompoo fruit
pigeon (Yin), resting in a native bottlebrush tree.*

AND ORCHIDS
DECK THE TREE TOPS,
AND FERNS THE WARM
DARK SOIL.

Home Birth

Damien Naughton, *oil on canvas, brush and syringe. Sydney gallery*

Damien's love of wombats inspired him to paint this work. He shows a mother wombat contemplating the miracle of marsupial birth. She licks a channel through her fur to spark her newborn's instinct to crawl into her pouch. Unlike our own technology-dependent births, the wombat's natural delivery represents the ultimate homebirth.[3]

CORE OF MY
HEART,
MY COUNTRY!
HER PITILESS
BLUE SKY

Meating Australians

Samantha Wortelhock, oil on canvas, brush and syringe. Private collection UK

On their six-day journey to Uluru, Samantha and Damien were astounded at how much of the country has been given over to stock animals and at the consequent degradation of the topsoil. Their route, along the ironically named Plenty Highway, was littered with squashed native animals forced to seek the few tender dew-fed shoots by the roadside.

WHEN SICK HEART
AROUND US
WE SEE THE
CATTLE DIE-

Last Supper at Uluru

Samantha Wortelhock, oil on canvas, brush and syringe. Private collection USA

*This dream-inspired work is probably the artist's most controversial painting.
She uses the image of the Last Supper to express her concern over the
continuing damage to our land. The hamburgers on the table indicate one
cause of this devastation. The fragile landscape has been damaged by the
herds of cattle which provide the meat for the burgers. While the Aboriginal
elder asks, 'Why?', the spirits of the now-extinct Tasmanian Tiger observe the
earthly events from a heavenly perspective.*

BUT THEN
THE GREY CLOUDS
GATHER
AND WE CAN
BLESS AGAIN

Hallelujah

Samantha Wortelhock, *oil on canvas, brush and syringe. Sydney gallery*

The rains come to the parched outback. Brolgas dance and baobab trees, like gospel-singers, raise their arms in praise to the pregnant clouds.

THE DRUMMING OF AN ARMY. THE STEADY SOAKING RAIN.

Cleansing the Heart

Samantha Wortelhock, *oil on canvas, brush and syringe. Sydney gallery*

During their last days at Uluru, the two artists were privileged to witness the rare phenomenon of rain 'at the rock'. The sight of huge volumes of water cascading in myriad waterfalls over its face was awe-inspiring. Samantha likened Uluru to a giant roof, collecting and then pumping the life force along well-worn channels into the surrounding desert.

CORE OF MY HEART,
MY COUNTRY!
LAND OF THE
RAINBOW GOLD,

Minga

Damien Naughton, *oil on canvas, brush and syringe. Private collection USA*

*Minga is an Aboriginal word for 'ants'. This painting was inspired by
a visit to Uluru and symbolises Damien's concerns about people walking
on this sacred rock.*

FOR FLOOD AND FIRE
AND FAMINE
SHE PAYS US BACK
THREE FOLD,
OVER THE
THIRSTY PADDOCKS,

Out the Back

Samantha Wortelhock, *oil on canvas, brush and syringe. Private collection USA*

*Under the purple hues of the vast Central Australian sky, a female
emu sits amongst the daisies, blue pincushions and spinifex, astonished
at the laying of her first egg.*

WATCH,
AFTER MANY DAYS
THE FILMY VEIL OF
GREENNESS
THAT THICKENS
AS WE GAZE...

Before Cutback
First in a trilogy

Damien Naughton, oil on canvas, brush and syringe. Private collection

Two cassowaries stand in a clearing surrounded by the rich colours of the rainforest – a vision of the perfect balance in nature which, Damien believes, must have existed before we began our systematic destruction.

AN OPAL-HEARTED COUNTRY, A WILFUL LAVISH LAND

Cutback
Second in a trilogy

Damien Naughton, *oil on canvas, brush and syringe. Artist's collection*

*A graphic portrayal of the devastation caused during a time when
loggers felled the forests without ceasing.*

ALL YOU
WHO HAVE NOT
LOVED HER,
YOU WILL NOT
UNDERSTAND-

Putting Back
Third in a trilogy

Damien Naughton, *oil on canvas, brush and syringe. Private collection*

Inspired by the artists' own work on their property 'Little Scrub' near Byron Bay. This piece depicts the regeneration of the forest by the planting of native trees – a difficult but fulfilling task. Overhead the spirits of the Cassowary observe the scene with the desire and the hope that they will reclaim their habitat one day.

THOUGH EARTH
HOLDS MANY
SPLENDOURS,
WHEREVER
I MAY DIE

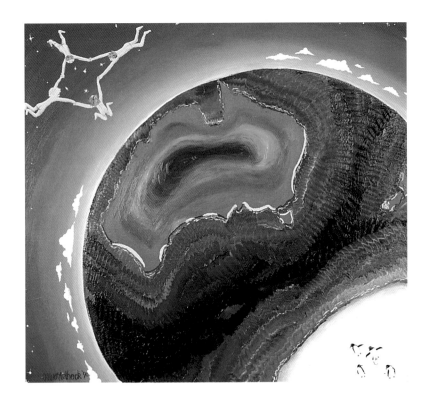

Free Fall

Samantha Wortelhock, *oil on canvas, brush and syringe. Sydney gallery*

The four figures in this innovative free fall sequence manipulate the Southern Cross as if it were a parachute. People's differing perceptions of Australia seem to disappear at this great height. As the power of objectivity works its magic, things appear connected and whole. Even the penguins stand in a Southern Cross formation.

I KNOW TO WHAT BROWN COUNTRY MY HOMING THOUGHTS WILL FLY.

Credits

1. Adrienne Howley, My Heart, My Country: The Story of Dorothea Mackellar, *University of QLD Press, 1989, p.78.*

2. Jane Roberts, 'My Dreaming Self' *in* The Unknown Reality, *Prentice Hall, 1977, pp.210-211.*

3. The artist acknowledges reference to the illustration on page 72 in Barbara Triggs's The Wombat, *NSW University Press, 1988.*

Restful Natives

Damien Naughton, *oil on canvas, brush and syringe. Sydney gallery*